THIRTY-SIX PSALMS

LET US PRAISE

Translated from the Hebrew & Interpreted by

BETTY BRACHA STONE

Copyright © 2014 by Betty Bracha Stone

All Rights Reserved

Published in the United States

ISBN 978-0-9960779-0-3

www.36psalms.com

Printed in the United States of America

Cover and book design by Richard Miles

In memory of Janet Adelman

beloved friend

CONTENTS

Index to the Psalms	*v*
Introduction by Betty Bracha Stone	*vii*
List of Psalms with altered sequences	*xi*
Thematic Index to the Psalms	*xi*
The Psalms	1 - 58
Afterword by J. Gerald Janzen	61
Glossary	62
References	63
Author's Gratitude	64
Designer's Note	65

THE PSALMS

Psalm One	1
Psalm Two	2
Psalm Four	4
Psalm Six	5
Psalm Twelve	6
Psalm Thirteen	7
Psalm Fifteen	8
Psalm Sixteen	9
Psalm Nineteen	10
Psalm Twenty-Three	12
Psalm Twenty-Seven	14
Psalm Thirty	16
Psalm Thirty-Nine	18
Psalm Forty-Two	20
Psalm Forty-Seven	22
Psalm Fifty-Seven	23
Psalm Sixty-Seven	24
Psalm Seventy-Seven	26
Psalm Eighty-Two	28
Psalm Eighty-Seven	29
Psalm Ninety	30
Psalm One Hundred	32
Psalm One Hundred Two	34
Psalm One Hundred Three	36
Psalm One Hundred Four	38
Psalm One Hundred Seven	41
Psalm One Hundred Twelve	44
Psalm One Hundred Fourteen	45
Psalm One Hundred Seventeen	46
Psalm One Hundred Eighteen	48
Psalm One Hundred Thirty	50
Psalm One Hundred Thirty-Seven	51
Psalm One Hundred Thirty-Nine	52
Psalm One Hundred Forty-Seven	54
Psalm One Hundred Forty-Eight	56
Psalm One Hundred Fifty	58

*The proceeds from this book support the school of
Kehilla Community Synagogue
in Piedmont, California,
the community that has nurtured
Betty Bracha's Jewish Renewal soul.*

INTRODUCTION

by Betty Bracha Stone

I began translating these psalms as a personal spiritual practice. Over the course of twenty-two months, the thirty-six psalms in this book became the vehicles by which I discovered a great deal about Hebrew, God, and myself. It came as a relatively late idea to share my renderings publicly. When that thought finally took hold, it came as an invitation that I want to extend to you: let us praise, grieve, and entreat together!

In the summer of 2012, I entered into a serious Jewish practice: strenuous introspection and prayer during the month of Elul in preparation for our High Holy Days – Rosh Hashanah and Yom Kippur. I'd often flirted with this custom but had never embraced it in rigorous fashion. That August, the time felt ripe, and I joined a group of Jewish women committed to supporting one another in this endeavor.

At our first meeting we sang a fragment from Psalm 84: "*Ashrei, yoshvai vaytecha*" – "Happy are they who dwell in Your home." As we sang in harmony with call and response, I was awakened by the poetry of the ancient Levites, the poets who wrote the words that would soon open for me a new connection to my Jewish spiritual life.

Our group embarked on the customary Elul practice of reciting Psalm 27 twice daily. So, the first morning of Elul, I settled down with the Psalm in Hebrew and in several English translations, ready to pray my heart out. Instead, I encountered the emotional reactions and issues I always had when reading the Psalms.

I was exalted. The poetry is stunning, the metaphors sublime. In Psalm 27, God is light, salvation, protector, and parent. God's path beckons me and God's home is my comfort. The words evoked in me an experience that was elevating, prayerful, and expansive.

I was angry. This psalm's world is divided into "us" and "them," with God weighing in heavily on our side. While Psalm 27 does not go as far as do other psalms by actually declaring that God will smash our enemies, it does imply that God and the psalmist are in complete agreement as to who those enemies are. My personal prayers do not divide up the world in this manner, so I was stymied. How could I pray this psalm?

I was confused. The Hebrew of the Psalms is so old that one cannot be sure that this psalm ever made complete sense, but for me in 2012 it certainly did not.

After painstaking efforts with the original Hebrew, the Brown-Driver-Briggs Hebrew and English Lexicon (2007), and many excellent translations, it became clear that all translators sometimes must take leaps to derive a coherent English text from the original Hebrew.

So there I was once again sitting with a psalm, exalted, angry, and confused. But this time I had to make it work as I had pledged to recite it morning and evening for six weeks. Psalm 27 and I were in a committed relationship. Jews are known as "God wrestlers," but I had not expected to square off with a representative of one of the most widely read pieces of literature in the world as part of my Elul practice.

This book is the result of that encounter. In translating these psalms into prayer, I have been humbled and transformed, moved and renewed by the exquisite language and the jarring challenges of the psalmists' ancient poetry.

My Guidelines for Translation

In order to translate Psalm 27 into English while retaining a prayerful mindset, I realized that I needed guidelines. What elements of the psalm could I vary? What must remain untouched? When had I gone too far and written my own poem inspired by an older and better one?

Here are the "rules" that gradually emerged over the ensuing months as I studied, grappled with, and prayed each of the thirty-six psalms.

I can tamper with time. The psalmists themselves varied the tense of the verbs within a psalm with surprising regularity and without discernable reasons for making a shift. Compared to English, the psalmist's sense of time does not refer to past, present, or future but rather distinguishes between action that is completed and action that is continuing. This afforded me considerable latitude in translating from their time sense into ours. Accordingly, I altered tense if it helped with the flow or the meaning of the psalm.

I can tamper with pronouns. Because we do not know exactly who was singing or praying these psalms or what their cultural understanding was in choosing pronouns, a door opened to interpreting the "I," "we," "you," and "they" referred to in the Hebrew. A change in pronoun was often all that was needed to move through the divisive "us" and "them" language of a psalm.

The psalmist most regularly refers to God using God's formal names יהוה and אלוהים (most often translated as LORD and God) or the pronoun "He." Changing these to

"You," or, even more intimately, "you," moved me, the human in prayer, into a more personal relationship with the Divine. The English "you" also eliminated the need to ascribe a gender to God, which was a relief.

I can tamper with the sequence of the verses. There are many eloquent aspects of the original Hebrew psalms which are lost in translation unless the translator is adept with the esoteric poetic devices found in Biblical poetry: internal alliteration or the common associations of certain words with other words. I found that parallelism – the repetition of meaning within the psalm – is a poetic device that does not translate well into English, however beautiful in Hebrew. Because of both my skill level and my purpose, my translations would not reflect these devices. I felt liberated to rearrange the order of the verses if doing so made a confusing psalm more coherent or if it allowed for the poetic expression of the psalm to flow more easily in English. There is a table at the end of this Introduction with a list of the psalms in which I have altered the sequences of the verses.

I can tamper with meaning.

Robert Alter (2007, p. 93) translates line 8 of Psalm 27 as,

> Of You, my heart said: "Seek My face." Your face, Lord, I do seek.

Even though I knew it would stretch beyond the limits of the Hebrew, I longed to interpret the line as an invitation to God: "Let us seek each other's faces." Because it was so gratifying to finally write that line, I became willing to interpret rather than translate when doing so strengthened my prayer.

This rule allowed me to portray "enemies" as internal shadowy misunderstandings of God's world, even though the original psalmist would surely look at me with disdain and confusion considering the real "enemies" who were dangerous and central aspects of his everyday life. To broaden the meaning for our time, I expanded the site-specific and people-specific references. Jerusalem became "our holy cities," and references to specific Jewish practice became something like "we follow our paths...."

I can tamper with some of the psalmist's assumptions about God. Because I wanted to pray to a God worthy of awe, supplication, and gratitude, I needed to liberate God from the most troublesome anthropomorphisms.

In the Psalms, God protects and comforts us. God is our guide and our haven.

God shines the light of clarity and love on us, chooses us, blesses us, and cherishes us. God also abandons us, allows our enemies to taunt us, turns from us, forgets us, and unleashes unfettered fury upon us.

I have no problem with most of these descriptions, as I see them as expressions of our earnest attempt to reach toward the Divine. But it was distressing to me when God's wrath was directed only against our foes. I did not want to carry on the projections of men long dead by participating in their sense of a justified rejection of the "other."

So when the God of the Psalms behaves in a socially destructive way according to my contemporary standards, I ascribe to myself, the human in prayer, all of the short-sightedness, vindictiveness, and petulance embedded in the psalm. I attribute the antisocial problems to us humans, and God gets a pass.

And why not? God, by definition, is beyond our understanding. We perceive this fact and yet stretch our souls and language toward a reciprocal, love-based connection with that which is unknowable. We are human. We are designed to make mistakes. God has abundant capacity to "bend down" in order to reach us. We are in this together – God and us. We seek each other's faces, and together, as in Psalm 57, we wake the dawn. Being able to pray from this perspective kept me going. Every psalm I translated offered me an opportunity to partner with the Divine. With this freedom of interpretation I happily immersed myself in the Psalms' gorgeous language and the psalmist's rich and palpable longing.

There are a few Hebrew words that I've retained in my renderings. These are words saturated with meaning for which I could find no equivalent in English. They are few in number: *Chuppah, Mitzvah, Selah, Shalom, Sheol, Shofar, Sukkah, Torah* and *Yah*. The Glossary at the back of this book contains my attempt at defining them.

My efforts at translating and interpreting these thirty-six prayers have allowed me to stand with those ancient psalmists, praising our Inspiration and our Source together. I have been raised up by their words and genius, and they come alive through my living breath. It is, indeed, our turn to grieve, entreat and praise. I am excited to have you join in.

Betty Bracha Stone
Oakland, California
May 29, 2014

Here is a list of the psalms in which I've altered the sequence of the verses: 4, 39, 47, 57, 67, 77, 82, 102, 104, 107, 118, 139, and 147.

As a quick reference aid to identify the major theme in a psalm, I have designated four major genres and which psalms fall more or less into each one:

"Praise": 16, 19, 23, 30, 47, 57, 67, 87, 100, 103, 104, 107, 112, 114, 117, 118, 139, 147, 148, 150.

"Supplication": 4, 16, 19, 27, 30, 39, 42, 57, 90, 130, 137, 139.

"Grief": 4, 6, 13, 39, 42, 77, 102, 137.

"Social obligation": 1, 2, 12, 15, 82.

Psalm One

Happy are we when we do not follow the misguided
Or stand with the confused
Or settle down with the scornful

When we delight in your teaching
We are not distracted from your truth

We are like a tree planted by flowing streams
We bear our fruit in its season
And our leaves do not wither
We succeed in all that we do

Not so the rootless.
They are like dried husks pursued by the wind.

The misinformed will not be able to stand in your court
Nor will the misguided keep company with the righteous
For you surely recognize the path of the righteous
And the way of the scornful will vanish into oblivion

Psalm Two

Oh God
My neighbors do not know me
And we growl at each other in the shadows

Earthly kings sit with princes of the realms
They gather against you and mutter about your "anointed one"
As they compete with each other for gold and bones

They conspire together saying,
"We are choked by God's stern laws.
We will break our bands and cast these chains from us.
We cannot be stopped."

You, enthroned in heaven, deride us:
"Did you, indeed, fashion yourselves?
Have you somehow determined that you will not die?
And, how do you know that you will not be judged?"

Your anger flares up against us
We feel the flames of Your fury and our chaos is terrifying

You say,
"I am sovereign.
It is I who anoints.
Look to my holy mountain
And to the holy places inside your hearts."

You say,
"See the baby, just born and already hungry in that devastated land?
She is my anointed, my own child.
Look to the left and to the right of you,
And behold my anointed, each one my own beloved heir.

Look carefully in your mirror,
And do not wonder where your blessings come from,
For you are my beloved, my own begotten child."

You say:
"Child, you only need ask and I will give you your inheritance,
Even to the very ends of the earth.
But you would rather shatter my treasure with staves of iron.
You destroy my gifts as if they are vessels that you yourself have shaped.

Now, therefore, oh you kings
Ponder this and be prudent.
Be chastised, you earthly judges.

I am to be served with awe.
You are to rejoice in me with trembling.
Treat my own anointed children gently.

Be careful lest you lose your way
And find yourselves in the path of my fury.

Happy are they who choose carefully and come to me for refuge."

Psalm Four

I call out to you
Oh righteous God
Answer me as I pray
Be gracious to me and loosen this binding pain

Cousins, neighbors, join me in holy service —
Why do you shame and dishonor me?
Why do you deceive me with empty love?
Don't you know that God chooses the compassionate?

God will listen as I cry out.
Cry out with me!
Be comforted with me.

We would do well to turn away from indifference
As you and I have only our righteousness to offer

Then we will find confidence in God,
Then our hearts will murmur to us as we surrender to sleep,
"Be still, Be quiet, *Shalom*."

Lift the light of your face to us, Oh God, that we might see Goodness
Put joy in our hearts as in the time of plentiful harvest
Turn our satiety into praise as in the time of newly pressed wine

When I lay me down, healing sleep is upon me
Because You, alone, are God
And because I dwell securely in Your home

Psalm Six

O God, don't let your wrath rebuke me
Don't let the heat of your fury burn me

Be kind to me, for I am depleted by grief
Heal me! I am dismayed to the bone

My soul is mightily vexed
Oh God! Oh God, till when?

Return my soul to me, O God, rescue me
Save me, as befits your loving kindness

As for me, I faint with weariness
Sighing all night, as if on my own bier

My tears are my best prayers
But I am drowning in these springs of grief

All my afflictions move me toward the grave
Surely, the dead do not remember you
And there is no gratitude in *Sheol*

Put away from me all effects of wrongdoing
So that you, O God, can hear the voice in my sobs

God, you hear and comfort me
God, you dwell in my prayers

All that would cause me to stumble has turned away

In an instant my shame is gone

Psalm Twelve

God, Help us
Loving-kindness has failed
And the faithful have vanished from among our children

Neighbor lies to neighbor
Vain flattery rolls from their lips
Even as they claim to speak heart to heart

Oh boastful language!
God will cut all your flattering smooth lips

The arrogant walk in circles and talk in riddles
They believe their own lies
While the needy are crushed by their words

They lift up the swift-tongued pretenders
And cannot recognize God in their neighbor's face

They say, "We are mighty of tongue
And our language makes us invincible.
Who is lord over us?"

God says,
"From the oppression of the poor
And from the groan of the needy
Now I will rise up.
I will protect them even as I ensnare those who puff about."

God speaks with purity
Like silver refined in the depths of this earth
Like pure metal melted seven full times

God will watch over the oppressed
And will protect them from this generation and forever

Psalm Thirteen

Until when, Oh God?
Will you forget me forever?
Will you hide your face from me forever?

Grief has taken hold of my heart;
How long will it counsel my soul?
How long will my enemy look down on me?

Show me, answer me;
Brighten my eyes, lest I succumb to the sleep of death,
Lest despair claim victory over me.

As for me, I have placed my trust in your mercy.
My heart rejoices in your deliverance
And I will sing to you because you have dealt bountifully with me.

Psalm Fifteen

Oh God
Like David, your servant
I long to live in your Temple
To dwell on your Holy Mountain

Show me the path and I will walk it with integrity
Show me the work and I will keep justice as my goal
Speak truth to me and I will open my heart to hear it

Keep slander from my tongue
Protect my neighbor from my thoughtless impulse
Silence my rebuke lest I accuse my dearest ones

Open my eyes that I may see the despicable melt from my vision
I will witness your glory
With eyes that were once sworn to the frozen, crooked path

I will not take advantage of the innocent
I will never turn my back on the needy

And so I am established in your Temple
And will never be moved. I am already home

Psalm Sixteen

Guard over me God!
I take refuge in you

I proclaim that you are my sovereign God
And that the only goodness I know is yours.
I proclaim that my delight is in all that is holy
And that this precious earth abounds in it.

There are those who rush around courting other gods
Their sorrows will surely increase
I will never make offerings of blood to those gods
Nor will I even pronounce their names

You, God, are my portion, my treasure, and my cup

Even when troubles befall me in pleasant places
Even in the dark hours when my very organs turn against me
You do not abandon me to the dark place.
You do not surrender the faithful to *Sheol*.

I will bless you, God, because you guide me

I have placed you before me forever
And I will never move
In this my heart rejoices
My body surrenders trustingly to sleep

God, show me your living path
And I will be replete with joy in your enduring presence

Psalm Nineteen

If we listen
The great arc of the sky will recount God's glory
And tell of Her handiwork

Daily the promise is expressed
And nightly wisdom is declared

But, unless we listen
There is no promise
And there are no words

God measures the measureless
Her words expand to the edge of the world
And there, she has established a home for the sun

The sun, like a bridegroom
Emerges in joy from his *chuppah*
And runs his path like a great hero

He appears at the edges of the sky
And his circuit includes the far reaches
Nothing is hidden from the heat of Her sun.

God's *Torah* is perfect, refreshing the soul
Her testimony is established
It makes the simple wise

God's teachings are straightforward and gladden the heart
Her *mitzvot* are clear
They enlighten the eye

Awe of God is pure and eternal
Her laws are true and altogether just

They are more desirable than gold
Than quantities of pure gold
And sweeter than honey dripping from the comb

We must guard them carefully because they are of the greatest consequence.

Oh God! Spare us from insolence
Let pride not rule us
We pray to be cleansed of arrogance and freed from great wrongdoing

Cleanse us even from those errors that are unknown to us
Make us, we pray, utterly blameless

May the words of my mouth
And the meditations of my heart
Be a reflection of your will
Oh God, my rock and my redemption

Psalm Twenty-Three

You, oh beloved friend, are my guide
I desire nothing more

We lie together in the fresh greens of spring
And you lead me straight to the quiet waters

You summon my soul into your embrace
And, in your sweet name, I walk the paths of righteousness

I fear nothing
For you are with me
Even when I walk in the Valley of the Shadow of Death
My power is yours and I will lean on your staff

I am comforted

You prepare a feast
And invite me to sit down with all my fears and demons
We receive your blessings and my cup overflows with joy

Oh! Goodness and kindness
Will surely keep me in their sight for all the days of my life
And it is in your house that I will rest for eternity

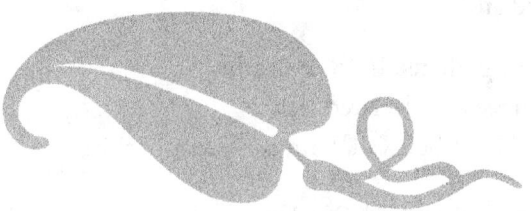

Psalm Twenty-Seven

A Gift from David

You are my light and my help
The strength of my life
Who else should inspire awe?

When evil came close to devour me,
My worst distractions and illusions,
They stumbled and fell

But even if they gathered in force nearby,
Even if they arose and declared war,
My heart would not be awed. I am confident of this.

There is only one thing I ask of you
I want to live in your home all the days of my life
To see your sweetness
And to visit in your Temple for that short time

When the day is dark, you hide me in your *sukkah*, like a treasure
You carefully secure me in the secret places of your tent

You lift me up onto a rock
And even though I can see my enemies circling around me
I am not distracted
I awaken to my practice with the *shofar* sounding in your own tent

I will sing and dance and play beautiful instruments
 In service to you I sing,
"Hear my voice when I cry! Be gracious to me, and answer me!"
With all my heart I say to you, "Let us seek each other's faces."

Don't hide your face and don't be angry
You have helped me, do not turn away from me, do not abandon me!
My father and my mother have left me alone in this world
But you will gather me in like a mother her brood

Sweet God, Show me your path
And lead me on an even road
Because there are those who lie in wait for me

Do not give me to my own passions and illusions
For they are great lies and will destroy me with a breath

If only I could strengthen my faith –
That it is possible to see your goodness in this land of the living –
Then I could wait for you with a strong and courageous heart
Then I could expect you

Psalm Thirty

Oh *Yah*, my God
I cried out to you and you healed me

I reached up to you and you bent to meet me
I am lifted up
And my enemies cannot touch me

You brought up my soul from *Sheol*
I did not die
And it is you who has done this

Moments come full of your anger
But life itself is your great gift

You, Oh God, have favored me mightily
You have made my mountain strong

But when you conceal your face
I am struck with terror

I cry out to you
And I bend low praying for mercy

What gain is found in my blood?
What profit will you find in my grave?
Will dust praise you?
Will dry bones speak of your truth?

Hear me, Oh God, and show me mercy
Help me! Rescue me!

Weeping comes to dwell in the evening
And in the morning, comes joy

You have turned my mourning into dancing
You have loosened my sackcloth and clothed me with joy

And so I declare that I will not be moved
I will not be silent
I will praise you

I will sing of your glory and of my gratitude forever
Sing God's praises you righteous ones
Remember the holy One with thanksgiving

Psalm Thirty-Nine

Oh God, I have loved my words
But now I watch lest they betray me
I must guard what I say
Because I am soon to die

Yah, You have robbed me of my voice
And sealed my mouth
Silence has struck me hard

I must hold my peace
But my suffering is great
And goodness does not approach

My heart burns within me
My meditation is consumed by the fire
And I must speak:

God! Stop afflicting me!
I am finished by the blow of your hand

You rebuke me for my foolishness
My beauty lasted a day and has melted like the moth's
I am only vapor
Selah

Yah, tell me of my end
Is this my last day?
I would know of my frailty

You have given me a life hardly worth the measure
Its duration does not register on your scale
We are all mist, established for the length of a breath
Selah

We walk the dusty road like shadows
And our plans are all in vain
Even when we heap up treasure
We do not know who will enjoy it

Now, where is my hope, Oh God
Except that it resides with You?

Deliver me from my failings
Do not make me the scorn of fools

Oh God listen to my prayer!
Give ear to my cry!
Do not respond to my tears with silence
I am a newcomer to you
As are we all -- just sojourners

Turn your sweet gaze toward me and I will find comfort
Then you will gather me into your dark embrace
Then I will go. I will be no more

Psalm Forty-Two

Like a deer thirsting for the brook
So my soul longs for you
God of all life

When will I arrive?
And how will I recognize your face?

Tears have been my only food
Night and day they mock me, saying,
"Where is your God?"

My memory is flooded
For I was once a pilgrim
With song and gratitude we approached your house
Eager to celebrate your holy day

But that was long ago
And now your home is abandoned
And I have lost my way

Oh my soul,
Why are you so despairing, clamoring to be heard?

> Daily, God expects loving-kindness
> And by night God sings to me of salvation
> Let me praise God
> Hold to that which is eternal

Oh God! My soul despairs within me
I remember the places of our encounters
All are ancient names on a dusty map
All is lost

In my depths
Voices of despair call out to one another
Like torrents
Like the breaking waves
They overwhelm me
Wash me away

> Every day, God expects loving-kindness
> And by night God sings to me of salvation
> Let me praise God
> Let me hold to that which is eternal

My heart is brought low, and my very bones call out murder!
All day they reproach me calling, "Where are you God?"

How can I answer?

> Daily, God expects loving-kindness
> And by night God sings to me of salvation
> Let me praise God
> Hold fast to the Eternal

Psalm Forty-Seven

Oh people! Clap your hands
And shout in triumph

God reigns from the heights of wonder
And Her power rings this earth

We are God's roar
And Her stamping foot

We are God's shout of ascension
And the voice of Her *shofar* is ours

God is the power of all this earth
We are the chorus and the song

Sing praises to God, sing praises!
Sing praises to the sovereign, sing praises!

God's delight is our inheritance
Those who went before us have secured Her love

Let us gather in the names of our ancestors
Let us become God's people,
Protected and inspired

The One is supreme ruler
And we are Her throne

We are The One's great exultation
And You, Oh God, are our shield and our comfort

Psalm Fifty-Seven

Be gracious to me, Oh God, show me mercy
My soul flees to you for protection

I take refuge under your wings
While calamity passes through the land

I call up to you, Oh God, most high
You, who completes me

I lie among the lions
Whose teeth are spears and arrows
And whose tongues cut like swords

Send down from heaven and rescue me
Send down your mercy and your truth
For they are panting to swallow me up

They have dug a dark pit and prepared a net to catch me
They have bent my soul low
But it is they who are ensnared, they who have fallen. *Selah*

You are higher than the heavens
And the whole earth is radiant with your glory

My heart is secure. You, Oh God have set it firm
I must give voice. Praise pours out in song

Infuse me with your glory
Inspire my harp
And together, let us wake the dawn

Among all peoples I show my gratitude
I give it voice in the midst of the nations

For while your loving kindness is great
And your truth reaches to the heavens,
You are higher than the heavens
And the whole earth is radiant with your glory

Psalm Sixty-Seven

God be gracious to us, and bless us!
Shine your face on us!
Selah

Oh, please make your path known here on earth
Grant all your peoples your steady guidance

May it be you who leads all the nations on this earth
And may we all rejoice with glad songs

May we all know the judgment reserved for the upright
Selah

The earth showers us with the abundance of your blessings
Through them, we, in turn, bless you to the extreme ends of the earth

All of us give you thanks
All of us!

Psalm Seventy-Seven

Oh God,
Give ear to my cries and listen to me
For on this troubled day
My hand has failed to find yours.
All night my pain flows without cease,
And my soul refuses all comfort.

You have seized my very eyelids
And I cannot close them.
My troubles have robbed me of speech.

The night sings a taunting song.
Is it my own heart I long to hear?
My own spirit that I seek?

When I pause to think
It is you I remember
And my moaning becomes a roar.
My soul is overwhelmed.
Selah

Have you cast me off forever?
Oh God,
Has your anger completely overcome your compassion?
My soul has abandoned itself to despair.

When I think of the days of your beginning
Those eternal years
Then I remember your great deeds
And dwell on your ancient wonders.

It was you who spoke of generations.
Is all that brought to nothing?
Has your loving-kindness completely withered?
You are the one who performed wonders.
You who announced your strength to all peoples.

When the waters saw you coming
They turned and trembled at the sight.
Even the deepest ocean quaked.

The clouds streamed forth water
Your thunder raged in the whirlwind
And bolts of lightning emblazoned the world.
The earth trembled and quaked.

Your way was in the water
Your path in the great seas
Where you left no footprint

Oh Eternal One, remember how you guided Moses and Aaron?
Remember how you shepherded your people through the wilderness?
Take my hand and lead me along this lonely path.
Soothe my brow with your breath
And whisper to me the song of my own soul

Psalm Eighty-Two

God
You stand among us
And witness how we mete out justice

You see that we allow the wicked to favor the wicked
And to adorn themselves with robes of honor

Let us plead on behalf of the poor and the orphan
Let us serve the destitute justly
Let us rescue the poor from the hand of the haughty

Until we do, we will never understand You
And will wander in darkness
As the very foundation of the earth shakes from the chaos

We are Your only agents, charged with Your judgment
And even the mighty among us will come to a human end
Let us look down from Your great heights
And remember our inheritance

Psalm Eighty-Seven

This is how to establish my holy mountain says the One:

Love your cities and burnish their gates
Dedicate all your dwellings to me
Call me by the name you hold most dear

There, in the heart of your lands
 I will be honored
And the earth will be full of my cities. *Selah*

I will mention Gaza and Beirut and Addis Ababa
As places I am to be honored

Add your own:
Frederichstadt, Riga, Atlanta, Gunthersville,
Iowa City, Gualala, Oakland,
And Jerusalem, always Jerusalem

Say of your home, this is where God's beloved child was born

Choose the place most holy to you and say of it:
This is where I was born
Where I received my birthright from the One on high

God will sign the city's register saying:
This is where my own beloved child has been born
It will be written in fire and love, in the language of the land. *Selah*

We will sing and dance
Joy will spring from wells of our blessed cities
And we will see it with our own eyes

Psalm Ninety

A prayer from Moses, a man of God.

Yah, you have been our refuge throughout our generations.
Before the mountains were born,
Before you brought forth this earth, this beautiful planet,
Even before eternity, you were God.

You revive us when we are crushed by mortality,
Saying to us, "You will surely return to me,
Since you were designed to die."

A thousand years are like yesterday in your eyes –
They pass like a single day,
Like the length of a watch in the night.

But we are swept away by the current of our days.
In the morning we grow like the grass,
We flourish and bloom.

By evening we are dried stalks waiting to be cut down.
And so we are faint in consideration of your rage –
Your fury terrifies us.

You have placed our transgressions before you,
Noting exactly what we wish to hide.
All our days circle around your wrath,
And we bring our years to their end with a sigh.

Why bother to count them?
If we are lucky, they number seventy; if we are strong, eighty years.
We spend them confounded by pride, trouble, and sorrow.
And then we are quickly gone; we just fly away.

Who can know the power of your anger?
Your wrath matches exactly our great fear of you,
Because it is you who awaits us.

So teach us how to count our days,
That we may find in ourselves our heart of wisdom.

Oh God, how long until you return to comfort us?
When you satisfy us in the morning with your grace,
We will rejoice and be glad all our days.

Even out the record.
Count the days of our suffering and grant us equal joy.

Let us serve you according to your great works.
Let us see our children bask in your splendor.
Let your great kindness rest sweetly upon us,
And on the work that is ours to perform.

Psalm One Hundred

A psalm of gratitude

Let us sing our praises out loud
The earth shouts along with us in triumph

We serve God gladly
And come into Holy Presence with joy
We know this – that *Yah* is sovereign
And that She made us for the purpose of being Hers
Her people, the flock of Her pasture

Let us come into Her gates gladly
And into Her courtyard with gratitude on our lips:
"We thank you God and praise Your name."

God is Goodness
Her loving-kindness is boundless
And She is faithful to us until the end of time

Psalm One Hundred Two

A prayer on behalf of the wretched, the downcast and the grieving:

Before you, Oh God, our suffering pours out like a fountain.
Yah, listen to our prayer. May it find no barrier.

Show me your face on this day of sorrow,
Listen to my cry and answer me quickly.

For my days disappear like smoke,
And my bones lie scorched in an angry heap.

I have eaten ashes and drunk my own tears.
I am weary flesh clinging to broken bones,
And sighs are my only voice.

I am a cormorant in the wilderness – an owl among the ruins.
I am a lonely sparrow keeping watch on the rooftop for my mate.

My enemies taunt me all day,
And those who once praised me are sworn against me.

You have been indignant and wrathful;
Now you lift me up, and now you cast me down.

You have confounded my strength and have shortened my days.
They are like a shadow in the failing light;
And I am withering like the grass in summer.

Oh God, do not take me in the middle of my few days.
You, Oh God, are established forever and remembered for all the generations.

You look down from your sanctuary
And behold, your work stretches from heaven to earth.
It is you who has built this blessed place,
You whose glory is apparent everywhere.

The peoples of this earth are awed by your name.
We gather to recount it in Zion and to praise you in all our Jerusalems.
We reclaim joy in the stones of your house – even in its dust.

Remember when you laid the foundation for this earth?
And formed the skies with your own hands?

Even when your creation is gone to dust and lost like an old cloak,
You will stand and you will make it all anew.

It is you who began it and who will sustain it;
You, whose years are measured by eternity.

You are moved by our prayer,
And have embraced the nakedness of our grief.

Now you will rise up,
Now you will listen to us.
You hear the prisoners' sigh, and throw open the doors of our cells.

The time has arrived to be consoled.
We are comforted in our service to you.
Our progeny are already secured in your plans.

Let this be written for now and forever.
We are created! We praise you.

Psalm One Hundred Three

My soul blesses you, Oh God
All that is within me blesses your holy name

My soul blesses you, Oh God
I never forget all that you have given me

You have overlooked my failings and healed my afflictions
You have saved me from darkest despair
And have crowned me with loving-kindness and sweet compassion

My hope is renewed within me
It takes flight and I am satisfied by goodness

You have made this known to us:
Your laws are on behalf of the oppressed
And our acts of justice belong to you

You are compassion itself
You are generosity and patience
You are the source of great kindness

When we contend with you
Your patience endures
Because anger has no foothold in eternity

It is not by our blemishes that you recognize us
And not by our great misdeeds that you deal with us

As far as the west is from the east
You have distanced our transgressions from us

As the heavens encircle the earth
So the strength of your mercy enfolds our fears

The comfort of your embrace is that of a compassionate mother

You know each bone of our skeletons
And remember the dust from which we are made

We are like the grasses that flower for a day
 Are kissed by the wind and then are gone

We will leave no lasting marker

But your loving-kindness is eternal to those who are aware of it
And your righteousness is already a boon to our children's children

Let us guard our understanding
Let us remember God's requirements
Let us do as we have promised

You have set your throne in the heavens
Your kingdom is all that is

Bless God all you angels, strong and bold
Listen to her words and do her bidding

Bless God all you hosts, you who administer her will

Bless God all creation, in all places and forever
My soul, planted deeply in all that is irredeemably and eternally yours,
Blesses you, Oh God

Psalm One Hundred Four

For the new moon

My Soul blesses you, Oh God, for you have grown very great
You wrap yourself with light like a cape
And stretch out the sky behind you
Like the curtain in your Holy Temple

Your home is made of the great waters
You stride on the wings of the wind
And the clouds are your chariot
They are your angelic messengers
And blaze up like fire to serve you

The earth, your Palace, is securely founded
It will never slip or fall

You established the deep waters above the mountains
And concealed their peaks with great seas

Then you set a boundary which the waters could not exceed
At your rebuke the seas fled
At your thunderous voice they trembled
And they never returned to cover the earth

The mountains rose up
The valleys sank down
To the places you established for them

You send springs into the gullies
Fresh currents flow between the mountains

You give drink to the mountains from your high seat
The earth is sated with the fruits of your work

Every beast of the field is given drink
The wild asses quench their thirst

You plant tall trees and provide for them abundantly
The stork nests high in the cypress
In the cedars of Lebanon, birds of the sky sing out their praise

The mountains are home for the wild goats
Their rocks are a refuge for the badger

You grow the grass for the cattle and green herbs for our service
Your bread fills our bellies and your wine makes our hearts glad
Our faces shine brighter than oil

You have appointed the waxing and the waning of the moon
And the sun knows when and where to set
You establish the darkness and it becomes night
All the creatures of the forest creep and glide under its cover

In the dark, the young lions raven and roar for prey
They seek their food from you, God
As the sun rises you gather them in and bed them down in their dens.
Then we come out to work, and are busy all day till evening

How great are your works, God!
You made all of us in wisdom
The earth overflows with your treasure

Here – the great seas are strengthened and widened
And creeping things without number find small creatures beside large ones

There – our ships on their way
And there – the great Leviathan, whom you created in order to play

All of us wait expectantly for you
Eager to be fed according to your cycles

You provide sustenance for us to gather in
You open your hand, and we are well satisfied

When you send your breath we are created
Your presence renews the earth

If you hide your face, we are dismayed

If you take our breath, we perish
And return again to dust

You touch the mountains and they smoke
You regard the earth and it trembles

God, Your glory is established forever
We rejoice in you as you do in us

I have sung to you all my life
I am singing still, and will never stop

My prayer is sweet in my mouth
I delight in you, My God

Help me see your world as undefiled
Let not my enemies take up residence in my heart

My soul blesses you Oh God!
All praises, all song, all breath!

Psalm One Hundred Seven

With full hearts
We thank you, Gracious One, for your eternal kindness

We are those whom you save from all danger
Whom you gather from the east and the west
From the north and from the sea
Who wander on a wild and desolate path
And have found no place to call home

In our anguish we call out to you
Ah! You guide us on a straight path
To a good place to live
Your kindness abides forever

We are those who sit in death's dark shadow
Bound in misery and iron
Rebelling against your words

But when we cry out to you
You deliver us from the grave
Lighting the corners where death lurks
And bursting our bonds asunder
Your kindness abides forever

You shatter the prison's bronze gates
And free us from its iron bars
But still, we choose a path of misery
Afflicting ourselves with our own wrongdoings
So that all food is abhorrent to us and we plan to starve

But when we cry to you
You satisfy us with a feast of goodness
You send your word, and it heals us
Your kindness abides forever

We go down to the sea in ships
And think to do business in great waters
But then we see your power in those treacherous depths
At your word, the storm winds stand and lift the waves
We are thrown to heaven, we descend to the depths
Our souls melt away in distress
And we reel like drunkards
All our bearings are swallowed up

But when we cry out to you in our anguish
You quiet the storm and still the waves
Ah, you guide us to a safe port
Your kindness abides forever

Rivers are transformed into wilderness
And springs into thirsty land
From a land of fruit into one of salt –
A sorry reflection of how we have lived here.
We find that we are barren, and are stricken with grief
Even as we continue our misguided ways
You pour contempt on those we choose to honor
And they wander in confusion, leading us nowhere

It is you who transforms the wilderness into a land full of springs
You who invites the hungry to live in this good place
To sow fields, and plant vineyards that yield sweet fruits

You lift us up in our need
And shepherd us toward comfort and plenty

We, who stand upright, see and rejoice
Injustice no longer speaks to us
We who seek wisdom will regard these things
And we will come to understand your love

Oh Gracious One
Your kindness is our breath
And the beat of our hearts
It is the rhythm of our days
And the quiet of our deepest dream
In your kindness we abide forever

Psalm One Hundred Twelve

Hallelujah
We are happy when we stand in awe of you, Gracious One
When our greatest pleasure is in your company

Our children will flourish
And their children will find a straight road to your blessings

Our homes will be abundantly full
Justice will be their corner-stones forever

As the sun rises to dispel the darkness
So, generosity, compassion, and righteousness beckon us to their light

It is good to remember that we are all borrowers
And that lending sustains your eternal laws

Then we will not quake,
Because God remembers justice forever

Evil tidings will not frighten us
Because our hearts are grounded in trust

You scatter your treasure among the needy
Your righteousness stands forever
The corners of your altar are raised up with honor

The trouble-makers see and are confounded
They gnash their teeth
Their lusts and their longings do perish

Psalm One Hundred Fourteen

When we came out from that land of slavery
Away from those people who stuttered and shouted
You envisioned our future in our own land
Judah and Israel as your holy dominion

The sea looked and drew back to let us pass
The Jordan changed its direction

The mountains skipped like rams
The hills like new born calves

What did it take for the sea to turn aside?
For the Jordan to change its course?

How is it that you mountains still leap like goats?
You hills, like spring lambs?

Before you, God, and in memory of those times, this earth will always tremble
Or shall we dare to call it dance?

You are our God
Who turns the rock into swamps and marshes
And the hardest stone into clear exuberant fountains

Psalm One Hundred Seventeen

Everybody!

Let's praise God together
Let's celebrate the Great Mystery
All of us

Because God's loving-kindness is overwhelming
And God's truth is eternal

Hallelujah!

Psalm One Hundred Eighteen

It is good to praise you, God!
Your kindness is eternal

Israel declares it:
Your kindness is abiding

Our priests proclaim it:
Your kindness is enduring

All who stand in awe affirm it:
Your kindness is everlasting

It is you I call when my spirit constricts
It is you who answers expansively

You know me and I am not afraid
What can people do to me?

Better to trust in you than to seek help from seekers
Better to trust in you than to take refuge in authority

I constrict and am surrounded by so-called nations
And, in your name, I rise to do battle
But you refuse to divide us according to our maps

I constrict and am besieged
And, in your name, I go out to cut them down
But you are unmoved, and leave me imprisoned

I constrict and they swarm around me like bees
I feel the fire of stinging nettles
And, in your name, I rouse myself to annihilate them
But you whisper a different message
And, battered and worn, I surrender to a new song:

"My strength and my song come from God
This will always be my salvation."

Even though you have rebuked me mightily, *Yah*
You did not surrender me to my own narrow vision

You lifted me up
And I have seen my enemies through your eyes!
It is wondrous in my sight

Indeed, I have not succumbed
I have lived to tell of your great works

This is the day that God has made
Let us rejoice in it gladly!
The tents of the righteous echo with gladness and salvation
God's right hand lifts me up and makes me strong

Open for me the gates of righteousness
I will enter them praising you:

"This is the gateway to God
Made for the righteous to enter
This is what lifts me up and makes me strong."

I praise you so that you answer me
You will always be my hope

Oh God please save me
Allow me to prosper

On that very stone that the builders rejected
Is founded the house of our God
Those who come in your name are blessed
We whom you bless, come into your home
And we whom you bless, go out to extend your blessings

Oh God who illuminates our lives
Bind us fast to your service
And secure us tightly to the corners of your altar

You are my God and I bless you
My God you lift me, even as I lift you

It is good to praise you, God!
Your kindness is eternal

Psalm One Hundred Thirty

From the depths I call out to you Oh God!
Listen to my voice

Give ear to this prayer of supplication
For you are my only hope

If you regard only wrong doings
Who would be left to stand before you?

Who would find comfort in your name?
And whom would you comfort?

Because you are forgiving by nature
Therefore I am awed

Because you are forgiving by nature
Therefore my soul awaits you

Because you are forgiving by nature
Therefore will I rely on your promise

My soul is yours
Those who keep watch from morning to morning know this
We have great hopes for you, Holy One

Because of your abundant mercy we are saved
You will redeem us and release us from all that threatens to subvert us

Psalm One Hundred Thirty-Seven

By the rivers of Babylon
There we sat and wept for our home
Our precious land

We hung up our harps and languished among the willows
Our captors mocked us and demanded our songs of Zion

How can we sing our holy songs in this stranger's land?

If I forget you, Oh Jerusalem,
May my right hand be forgotten, for it belongs to you
And may my tongue adhere to the roof of my mouth
If I do not set Jerusalem above my greatest joy

We have sworn in our hearts to never forget
We have sworn in our hearts that revenge is sweet
We are lost

These strangers will surely be brought to waste
We are lost

Their children will surely suffer as ours do
We are lost

No one is safe from the sharp rocks of memory
We are all strangers blinded by our tears

Oh God, keep their babies safe. And ours.
Find us, Oh God, find us!

Psalm One Hundred Thirty-Nine

Oh God, You have searched me
And You know
How I sit down and how I get up

You discern my purpose from afar
You are accustomed to my ways
And observe all my habits and lusts

Not a single word forms on my tongue
Except You already know it

Where would I go from Your spirit?
Where would I flee from Your presence?

If I should ascend to heaven
You are there
If I make my bed in the under-world
Behold, You are waiting

If I soar on the wings of the dawn
Or settle at the furthest edge of the sea
Even there, Your hand would lead me
Your right hand will not let me go

All I can say is that this dark place overwhelms me
Night and light swirl around me
And argue for my soul

But the darkness does not create terror
In Your presence, night shines like day
And the blackest place is illumined

You, Oh God, have grabbed me from out of nowhere
And have put Your hand upon me.
And so I am formed.

Your designs are without number
And there is no limit to them
Their number is greater than the sand

These matters are too lofty for me
I am unable to understand such wondrous things

I declare that I am one of Your wondrous works
That I am fearfully and wonderfully made

Your eyes saw my unformed self
It is You who described me in the Book well before the days of creation

My essential structure was not hidden from You when I was fashioned in secret
And artfully woven in the lowest parts of the earth

This my soul knows right well
Even my organs are Yours
Because it is You who wove and protected me in my mother's belly

I imagine You slaying the wicked, those men of blood done away with—
They, who (surely not I) utter Your name with wicked thought
They, who (surely not I) slander You

I absolutely abhor those who abhor You
I damn those who damn You
And do I not strive against those that rise up against You?

I find I am unable to stop myself
I count them as my enemies
And I hate them with utmost hatred!

Search me, Oh God, and know my heart
Try me, and know my thoughts

Reveal to me the way You know me
Knit for me all my parts –
Even those I wish to hate

Show me how You see the parts that seem grievous
Show me how You love them
Hold me fast dear God, and set me free
Lead me on Your eternal path

Psalm One Hundred Forty-Seven

Hallelujah!

We sing to God with gladness
For our joy is pleasing and our praise beautiful

The One, with limitless understanding
Counts every star
Summoning each by its own name

God's word runs swiftly
And covers the whole earth
God speaks through snow, white as wool
And frost that blows about like ash

Who can stand before this cold?
This ice that pelts us like crusts of bread?

God speaks
And the frost melts
The winds stir and the waters swell

The skies cover themselves with clouds
Preparing the earth for rain
The mountains spring to life with grasses

God feeds the beasts
And the children of the ravens

God finds no delight in the might of the horse
Nor any pleasure in human muscle

Rather, You turn toward those who turn toward You
Who wait for Your compassion

You testify on behalf of the homeless
And cast the arrogant down to the earth

Healer of the broken hearted
You bind up our wounds

You build a home for the outcasts
And gather us into its holy shelter

We respond with thanksgiving
And sing praises with our instruments

Let us praise You, God, from our sacred places

For You have secured us in our towns
And blessed the children in our midst

You brought peace to our borders
And satisfied us with the finest wheat

You declared Yourself to those who revered You
You give Your laws and judgments to us, their descendants

We believe You have not done this with others
We think we are the only ones who understand Your teachings –
Your patience is boundless

Hallelujah!

Psalm One Hundred Forty-Eight

Hallelujah!
Praise the One!
The sky shouts praises
While angels and all the heavenly hosts sing out

Oh, praise the creator of those high realms
The sun! The moon! Those stars of light!
The sky of skies and the waters that are above them

Oh, praise the creator of this planet
All dragons and creatures of the great deep seas
Thrash about in praise
Because it was God's intention that established them forever

Fire, hail, snow and mist!
The great winds storm to do God's bidding

The mountains and all the high places rise to glorify
The fruit trees and the tallest cedars send up their limbs to praise

The animals of the plains and the desert
The ones in our pens and the ones who still roam wild
The ones that creep and glide
The ones that soar on broad wings
They all exalt the One whose imagination brought them forth

The kings of this earth, the princes, ministers and judges
The peoples of cities and of the lonely desert
The boys and girls running for the joy of it
The babes toddling in circles
And we whose strength has waned

All of us everywhere
We all praise the name of the Creator
The earth and the heaven are resplendent mirrors of the One

The One has summoned us with the great horn
We are all held fast by God
The ones who praise, chosen for praise

Psalm One Hundred Fifty

Hallelujah.
Can you hear me?
Hallelujah!!

Let's praise God from this Place.
Let's do it on top of Mount Moriah,
And from the banks of the Ganges.
Let's do it from attics with crosses on the wall,
And from basement rooms with incense and reed mats.

Let's praise God from the sacred groves,
And while swimming in the coral reefs.
Let's dive into the springs of New Zealand
And emerge in the ice caves of the tundra.
Let's praise Her from the eagle's nest
Where the clouds gather in a blue sky.
Let's climb Kilimanjaro and shout.

Let's wake up the neighbors and exhaust ourselves with praise!

Let's praise God for the abundant.
For hills and rivers, mountains and trees.
For the great waters, the blizzard and the monsoon.
For the sands of the desert and for the winds that raise them to storm.
For mighty forces - the typhoons and tornadoes, the earthquakes and volcanoes.

Let's praise God with the blast of the *shofar* —
The trumpet, the tuba, and bassoon —
The wind horns and the reeds.
Bring your flute and your piccolo – they will be heard.

Let's praise God with the lyre and the harp –
The zither, guitar, and mandolin, the banjo, and ukelele.
If you know what a psaltery is, bring it!

Get out your drums and timbrels –
The rik, the zills and the cow bell.
Beat the great djembe, the dumbek and the trash can lid.
The tambourine is also good.

Let's get down and do some dancing.
Let's cavort and leap – in circles and in lines,
Together and with our eyes half closed.
In touch with the great rhythm, let's get wild and breathless.

Let's raise the decibel level with cymbals –
Let's ring the great bells.

Let's jump and hoot,
And summon all life.

Let's sing and bray and bark and roar. Let's honk.
And snort and cavort in the green meadows.
God will surely hear us. She will surely join in.
There will be rainbows and waterfalls, lightning and thunder.
The Northern Lights will dance for us and the stars will pulse to our beat.
There will be love and joy and justice.

We who breathe share a soul designed to praise –
The Conductor,
The Choreographer,
The Designer.
It is what we do. It is how we are made.

AFTERWORD

J. Gerald Janzen
MacAllister-Petticrew Professor of Old Testament, Emeritus
Christian Theological Seminary, Indianapolis, Indiana

The Book of Psalms, the longest book in the Bible, is filled with all manner of things that we human beings are encouraged to say to God. Surprisingly, the majority of these words are questionings, complaints, even downright accusations that God has not done right by us. But when we look at the book of Psalms as a whole, it displays a direction in the development of its themes, from the dominance of question and complaint to the dominance of thanksgiving and praise.

These last themes do not arise easily, nor are they sustained steadily. Like salmon swimming upstream toward their headwaters, thanksgiving and praise arise against the strong opposing current of all that so often goes wrong in human life. Yet, in the end, the Book of Psalms wins its way to a final group of psalms that are filled with unbroken praise.

This trajectory toward "praise" is clearly present in this collection. And it is fittingly noted in the subtitle, as Bracha invites us to join her: "Let Us Praise!"

I find her translation technique and her idiom innovative in their contemporary freshness, and yet deeply conservative: based on careful study of the Hebrew originals and personal engagement with them through prayer and meditation, these re-voicings carry forward the vibrant, honest piety of the original writers. And further, they carry the prayerful reader to a place where all those who have prayed or sung these psalms join in one chorus.

Writing as a Christian in the Anglican tradition, where the Psalms form an integral part of daily and Holy Day worship, I celebrate Bracha Stone's achievement especially for its concern to transcend the "we/they" thematics of many of the original psalms. Throughout her translations she is attuned to the spirit of Psalm 150 where "We who breathe share a soul designed to praise." We're all invited to praise. It is when we are willing to sing together that we may become able to live together; and these translations will provide a fine vehicle for such ventures of oneness-in-difference. Truly, these translations by Betty Bracha Stone offer a means of *berakhah*, of blessing, to many.

Glossary

Chuppah: Four poles holding up a prayer shawl, under which a couple stands in order to marry. It symbolizes the home that the couple will build together, and, like the *Sukkah*, is notable for it's fragility.

Mitzvot (plural of Mitzvah): Comes from the root meaning to command and literally refers to precepts and commandments given by God in the *Torah*.

Selah: There is no consensus as to the meaning of this word. It occurs in the Psalms where "amen" might occur or where a musical notation might be present. It could simply represent a marker for a pause. I love that no one knows what it means. Selah!

Shalom: Translates as "peace" and comes from the root that implies completion.

Sheol: The name for the place where we go after death. It is dark, deep, unpleasant, and is not described with specific details.

Shofar: A ram's horn used by the ancient Israelites in religious ceremonies, to announce the new moon, and as a summons to gather or to battle. It is still sounded during the period of Rosh Hashanah and Yom Kippur.

Sukkah: A temporary and fragile shelter designed to let the elements pass through it. It reminds Jews of our period of wandering and suggests the difference between the insecurity found in our own efforts and the security found in the love of the Divine.

Torah: Literally means the first five books of the Jewish Bible, but more often, means all the teachings and moral injunctions that Jews take on as having come from God.

Yah: A commonly used name for God, as in "Hallelu-Yah." It derives from the pronunciation of the first two letters (יה) of the unpronounceable four-letter name for God (יהוה). It is spoken with an out-breath and I think of it as a spiritual sigh.

References

Robert Alter. *The Book of Psalms.* Norton: New York, 2007.

Francis Brown, **S.R. Driver & Charles A. Briggs**. *The Brown-Driver-Briggs Hebrew and English Lexicon.* Coded with Strong's Concordance Numbers by Hendrickson Publishers: Peabody, MA., 1906 & 2007.

Matityahu Clark. *Etymological Dictionary of Biblical Hebrew.* Based on the Commentaries of Rabbi Samson Raphael Hirsch. Feldheim Publishers: Jerusalem, 1999.

Betty Bracha: Bracha is the Jewish name that my parents gave me at my birth. It means "blessing" in Hebrew. Betty is the English name they gave me because it began with the same consonant as Bracha and appeared "American" to them in Atlanta, Georgia in 1944.

Cities found in Psalm 87: My maternal grandparents came from Frederichstadt and Riga. I was born in Atlanta and have lived in Gunthersville, Iowa City, Gualala, and Oakland.

Gratitude

I am grateful to those who supported me in this project.

*Kehilla Community Synagogue provided the loving context
in which such an idea as to translate a psalm for myself could take root.
It also provided the opportunity to begin to share my translations with others.*

*Rabbi Dorothy Richman convened and led the Elul group that
started this project.*

*Linda Blachman and Rachel Stone
generously gave editing advice.*

*Richard Miles graciously offered to do the heavy lifting
that has brought this project to fruition.*

My family, friends and dog encouraged and loved me.

*And, of course, my husband, Don,
walked this path with me, just as he always does —
this time in the guise of editor extraordinaire.*

Designer's Note

When Betty Bracha Stone shared the first of her Psalm translations with me, she was simply offering to share her deep and authentic spiritual experience with a fellow congregant, Biblical Hebrew translation fan, and long-time friend.

As a poet, I appreciated the Psalms as I knew them, mostly via the lyrical verses of the King James version. But they really weren't for me. Until now. Bracha's translations make them accessible and highly relevant way down in my Jewish soul. I was touched and inspired and suddenly felt that the Psalms might have some spiritual, and not merely poetic, meaning for me today.

I could see she was about to embark on a path that would wend its way through scholarship, art, feeling and spirit and I offered, once a collection happened, to design the book that they would become. I knew that at that time she had no inkling she was creating a book, but as the song says, "Hey, look at us now."

Don Stone, Bracha's husband, was an untiring partner in the last months of designing and editing. He persevered, as only he can, to make sure that every aspect of this book conveyed the intention of the author and received the editing to accomplish it.

I am really touched to have the honor to take her work and put it into physical (and digital) form for people to experience, and am humbled that Bracha trusted me enough to put the fruits of her labor into my hands.

Bracha wanted cover art that was green and full of life. The cover photo was taken in the Southern Highlands of Tanzania, an unspoiled mountainous region overlooking Africa's Great Rift Valley and the cradle of humankind. The road where this was taken does not appear on Google maps, but I can assure you there is indeed a road, one need only trust that they can find it.

Richard Miles
Dar es Salaam, Tanzania
May 2014

www.ingramcontent.com/pod-product-compliance
Lightning Source LLC
Chambersburg PA
CBHW060530010526
44110CB00052B/2549